DRAINING THE SWAMP

A PLAY BY

D.R. HILL

Draining the Swamp
Third Edition
Copyright © 2020 by D.R. Hill
All rights reserved.

ISBN#: 978-1-7396863-7-6

No part of this book may be reproduced, scanned, or distributed in any printed or electronic form without permission. Performing rights to this play can be obtained from DRH Arts Ltd (company number 11793105, registered in England and Wales). Registered office and business address – 1 Craufurd Rise, Maidenhead SL6 7LR, UK

www.drharts.org   drhartsltd@gmail.com

Dixon and Galt LLP

Draining the Swamp

By D.R. Hill

The premiere of the play was given by The Company at the Edinburgh Fringe Festival from 16-27 August 2023, in a reduced version. The performances were at C Arts Aquila, Temple Theatre. Subsequently the full play was presented at Norden Farm Centre for the Arts in Maidenhead from 28-30 September 2023.

The cast in Edinburgh and Maidenhead was as follows:

Sir Oswald Mosley	Rowland D. Hill
Lady Diana Mosley	Tina Thomas
Cimmie and Baba	Georgia Winters
Curzon, Joyce and Frost	Simon Polo-Clarke
Jeffrey, Syers and Tarrant	Dawson James

Directed by	Su Gilroy
Lighting and Technical Design	Matthew Biss
Stage Manager/Technician	Robert Bullen
Rehearsal photographs	Paddy Gormley

In 2024 a second production of the play toured venues in London and south-east England. The cast and creative team was as follows:

Sir Oswald Mosley	Rowland D. Hill
Lady Diana Mosley	Ciara Pouncett
Cimmie and Baba	Claudia Whitby-Tillott
Curzon, Joyce and Frost	David Boyle
Jeffrey, Syers and Tarrant	Chris Keyna
Directed by	David Furlong
Designed by	Jeffrey Choy
Lighting/Technical Design	Matthew Biss
Technical/Stage Manager	Robert Bullen
Production photographs	Paddy Gormley

The Company would like to thank Norden Farm Centre for the Arts for its support for this production.

Characters (played by five actors):

Actor 1 - Sir Oswald Mosley (age 65)

Actor 2 - Lady Diana Mosley (age 51) and other roles

Actor 3 - Cimmie Mosley (nee Curzon) and Lady Alexandra Curzon (Baba) (age 32), Speaker of the House and other roles

Actor 4 - Tory MP, Lord Curzon, William Joyce, Police Officer, Prison Guard, David Frost

Actor 5 - Jeffrey Hamm, Labour MP, Waiter, Cecil Syers and Brenton Tarrant

Design

The play has been presented with different design ingredients, and it is open to any creative team to determine the style of presentation. However, the intention is that there should be a large projection screen upstage, used throughout the production for both still images reflecting the location for each scene (including a title identifying location and date), and edited historical moving image to provide transitions between scenes. Moving image is available for use with any production, subject to appropriate royalty payment.

Prologue — Welcome to La Temple de la Gloire — Friday 6 October 1961

(As the audience enter there is a projected image of the ornate outside of the Mosley house in Orsay, France, and the buzz of recorded voices at a modest reception)

(Actors 4 and 5 can take tickets as the audience enter, as if checking invitations to the event)

Scene 1 — The Mosley house, Orsay, France— Friday 6 October 1961

(Auditorium door closes, lights go down, initial moving image news reel drawing us back to 1961)

(Then, projected image of the house at Orsay as for the Prologue. The location and date now appear projected on the image – The Mosley house, Orsay, France – Friday 6 October 1961)

(Actors 3, 4 and 5 may enter stage as guests at the reception, actor 4 playing the role of master of ceremonies)

Actor 4   Ladies and gentlemen. Please welcome our host and the Leader of the Union Movement, Sir Oswald Mosley.

(Oswald enters in a bow tie and jacket, theatrical entrance. Diana is with him).

Oswald   Good evening and welcome to our home, the Temple of Glory, for this special occasion to celebrate the launch of the new Union Movement, and… our twenty fifth wedding anniversary!

(Applause, both recorded and from actors on stage)

This day is momentous and will be remembered in years to come. We are looking forwards. We are looking at The Alternative, (Holds up his new book) a new way of thinking that will bring an era of political change.

I know that you all believe, like us, that we are Europeans together and that we should drive forwards a purposeful vision for a united Europe, where national boundaries are broken to allow free trade and free movement. That can only make economic sense. There must be no more wars on European soil.

Next year, I will be chairing a "Europe One Nation" conference in Venice. It is a bold and vigorous idea that is beyond both traditional democracy, and fascism. This is a new beginning! The rest *will* follow.

(Applause, recorded as needed, supported by the actors. Jeffrey steps forward with two glasses of champagne. Hands one to Mosley)

Jeffrey   When are you coming back home, Oswald?

Oswald   When I'm ready. I won't be rushed. We need to stand back, take considered decisions. The focus has to be the fight for European Union.

Jeffrey   What about the fight for Britain.

Oswald   That's also what we're fighting for.

Jeffrey   Where's the old impatience, the urgency to get things moving? Venice is fine, but we need you back home. People are hungry to hear you speak again, to hear you attack the immigration peril. Britain is being flooded with impoverished Blacks.

Oswald   But look around you Jeffrey.

(Pause)

Where are the reporters? The BBC won't give me broadcast time. Communication is about more than public meetings. If only there was an alternative to the press. Can you imagine a time when mass communication is freely available, no censorship by default? Think what that would mean. My voice could really be heard.

Jeffrey Your voice can be heard! Through the meetings the support will grow, especially if the party adopts an aggressive "No Blacks" policy.

Oswald How many times do I have to tell you that the Union Movement cannot be racist? We must be about equality for all.

Jeffrey That's your ideal. It's not what the people think. We have to listen to them. It's a fight and you're needed on the podium. Next election, we can win Notting Hill. Canvassing starts now! There's a battle to be won…. and this time we will drive through Cable St.

Oswald Cable St.! The past. The future is building prosperity for all, across the Commonwealth. That's the way to stop immigration.

Jeffrey Be real.

The membership needs you to come back into the field. Are you up for it…or, are you finished?

(Diana interrupts them)

Diana I hope you two are not going to fight.

Oswald	Just fetch my stick will you Diana, and I'll show my friend here that I do still have it in me (he adopts a mock fencing posture).
Jeffrey	It's your skill on the platform that is needed, not your fencing prowess. People listen to you. They always have.
Diana	Jeffrey, come and meet David and Wallis.
Jeffrey	But think about it! You can't hide away here. Great Britain needs you.
	Congratulations on the silver anniversary though. Well done…to both of you.

(Jeffrey exits with Diana)

Oswald	(To himself) Twenty-five bloody years.
	They come so quickly.
	How much time is left?
	Are you finished? Really? Are they right?
	When the moment comes, the call, will I be able to respond? Can I still do it?

(He sees Cimmie in the audience, 1930's white night clothes, ghost-like. Oswald is entranced)

> Cimmie?
>
> Cimmie! Is that you?
>
> Cimmie, my darling.
>
> Come to me.

(She steps onto the stage but keeps distance, circling. It's like a game and she keeps the same distance between them, wherever Oswald moves)

You are as beautiful, and as desirable as ever.

Come to me.

We were always made for each other.

Come into my arms.

I can do it with you, Cimmie. I can change the world. I can do anything.

(He gradually wins her over, reluctant at first, she relents and comes to him, drawn as to a magnet. They are together. Perhaps they kiss. She may remove his jacket leading us into the next scene and change of time period)

I will go back to England. I'll take them on again.

(He becomes focused on his own thoughts. She slips away and exits)

I can do anything. I always could.

It's the fire inside, just as I remember

(Transition projection with edited news reel taking us back to 1931)

Scene 2 — Houses of Parliament — 6 October 1931

(Projected image of the inside of Westminster Hall, the Houses of Parliament, with location and date for scene, Houses of Parliament, 6 October 1931)

(Actors 4 and 5 enter to either side of the stage, establishing Tory and Labour benches. Actor 3 becomes the Speaker of the House. Actor 2 playing Diana may also contribute heckling and "hear-hear" as a member of the Tory benches. Sound effects of the typical House of Commons uproar)

Actor 3	Order! Order!
	The Right Honourable Sir Oswald Mosley
Actor 5	The perfumed popinjay of scented boudoirs! (Laughter)
Actor 3	Order! Order!
Oswald	Yes, you may well sneer, you men of inaction. You who determinedly sit by and do nothing whilst the people of this country labour for impoverished wages or suffer the indignities of unemployment.
Actor 5	Hear-hear. Let's have some leadership.
Oswald	I offer you a vision for the working people of this great country. It's Revolution by Reason. A vision of equality, where wages are fair, working hours

acceptable, where unemployment does not exist, and there is decent housing for all.

Actor 4 Betrayer of your class.

Actor 3 Order! Order!

Oswald We need an emergency programme to meet the immediate unemployment crisis, and then a long-term policy to reconstruct our industrial life.

Actor 4 He wants a revolution!

Oswald We can provide employment for eight hundred thousand through new construction projects. A mobile labour corps will tackle slum clearance.

Actor 5 And who's paying for this? You'll bankrupt the country

Actor 3 Order. Order! (Noise)

Oswald I can answer that. I can answer that. The money will be raised by loans against the revenue of the Road Fund. Are the people of this country not worth that investment? They are.

Actor 5 Hear-Hear!

Oswald Longer term we need a commitment to Imperial socialism. To maximise the trade market of the Empire.

Actor 4 What we want is a bigger export economy. More Exports. More Exports (chanted by all, Tory and Labour consensus).

Oswald No! No. We must put new money into the right hands. Give to working families not to the producers.

Actor 4 It's communism by any other name!

Actor 5   The pronouncements of a madman!

Oswald   Government must be about action not words. No more deliberate vacillation leading this country into decline.

Government should serve the people, not the rich and powerful, not the Jewish financiers and the industrialists.

Actor 5   He wants to run before he can walk.

Actor 4   It's madness.

Mosley   The failure of the Labour Party to support the working people of this country is an abomination.

Actor 4   Well, Come back to the Tories then!

Mosley   Never! We need new politics in Great Britain. A new party. I walk away from Labour (other actors leave the stage) and will lead my New Party to electoral success. We will show you what the will of the people means. For Britain, the Empire and the working man.

(Diana appears and there is a moment between her and Oswald, perhaps the keys to the flat are passed over and they kiss. Actor 4 becomes Lord Curzon)

Curzon   Mosley, a word.

If I didn't respect your mother, I'd take a horsewhip to you.

Oswald   Charming.

Curzon   Have you any idea of the distress you are causing my daughter?

Oswald   This is hardly the place.

Curzon	Oh, and where is the place. You're never at your home. You are either giving speeches or you're at a party somewhere.
Oswald	And very good they are too. The parties I mean.
Curzon	You complacent bastard. Is marriage meaningless to you?
Oswald	On the contrary, Cimmie means everything to me. I couldn't live without her.
Curzon	Is that why you sneak around with the Mitford woman?
Oswald	Lord Curzon, I can't help it if I'm popular. I don't seek that kind of adoration, but I seem blessed to receive it.
Curzon	Are you denying your affair.
Oswald	I'm denying the harm.
Curzon	Cimmie is ill, Oswald. You should be caring for her, being a husband, not playing the dilettante and holidaying in the Mediterranean.
Oswald	My visit to Italy, if that's what you mean, was entirely one of political business. And very informative it was too. Have you any idea of what is being achieved in that country. If only we had the courage to act like Mussolini.
Curzon	He's a fascist
Oswald	Of course, so was Caesar. It's in the Italian blood. And Rome had an Empire, as we have for the moment, but seem keen to lose.
Curzon	Oswald, you have been a member of every political party in this country, including your own.

	It's failed. You're never going to be Prime Minister. Be realistic. I urge you to focus on your wife, on your family.
Oswald	Thank you for your advice, Lord Curzon.
	Glad to know you think my political career is finished. I happen to think it's just starting. And the word fascist, which you seem so cynical about, is actually a very apt way to describe where my beliefs are, based on the success of that approach in Italy and the total and utter failure of our own Parliamentary system.
Curzon	Failure? Because you and your ideas have been rejected?
	You will lose the respect of everybody who's ever supported you. The establishment will turn its back on you. And Cimmie will have nothing to do with fascism!
Oswald	Wrong again, Lord Curzon. I have already shared with Cimmie my plans for another new party. And it really helps my thinking to know the establishment is running so scared of that. You will have played your role in convincing me of the need to launch the new British Union of Fascists!

(Mosley exits. Curzon is left, unable to respond, then exits)

(Transition edited news reel moving from 1931 to 1932)

Scene 3 — The home of Oswald and Cimmie Mosley, Savehay Farm, Denham — July 1932

(Projection of an image of the interior at Savehay with title of the location and date for the scene - The home of Oswald and Cimmie Mosley, Savehay Farm, Denham — July 1932)

(Cimmie is in a nightgown. She nurses the baby who is six weeks old)

(Oswald enters. He removes his bow tie and opens a top button. He hasn't been home since the birth of the child)

(Pause)

Cimmie   This is Michael, Oswald.

(Oswald approaches)

Oswald   He doesn't look much like me!
Cimmie   Thank God for that
Oswald   What do you mean?
         (Pause)
         He is mine?
Cimmie   How can you say that?
         What I meant was that I don't want him growing up to be like you.

	To treat women the way that you do. To treat me the way that you do.
Oswald	I adore you Cimmie and I'm sorry if I've been particularly busy lately. It's a challenging time. Of course I'm delighted with Michael. Let me hold him.
Cimmie	No. He's settled now.
	I'm not getting much sleep.
	It's what you've been busy with though Oswald.
Oswald	Establishing the party is not easy. I need more help.
Cimmie	You've recruited Baba, I see.
	She's seeing a lot more of you than I am.
Oswald	Your sister is very supportive. And she's bringing in other women from our set.
Cimmie	Yes, I can imagine they are keen to be in close proximity to Oswald Mosley.
Oswald	Oh Cimmie, when are you going to stop this constant jealousy.
	The sooner you can be back with us, on the platform, the better.
Cimmie	I'm not sure about that Oswald. I'm not convinced that fascism is the way forward. There's a violent side to this that does not accord with my values and with the kind of society I want to see. I thought we shared strong principles of fairness and equality.
Oswald	Of course we do. The commitment, for both of us, has always been to improve the conditions of

working people, working families. That remains the vision.

(Pause)

You can play such a role in this Cimmie. Once Michael is weaned. And with the support of your sisters. I need you back with me, in the field.

You've no idea how popular you are.

Cimmie The thing is Oswald, how can I trust you?

I can't bear to hear the whispers, to see the knowing looks exchanged between people I call my friends. And now Baba is…

Oswald What about Baba! For goodness sake you don't think….

Cimmie How can I trust you?

I don't see you for weeks on end. I don't know what you're up to. Who you're seeing in that flat in Ebury St. Why do you need that anyway?

Oswald This has got to stop Cimmie. You're tearing yourself apart for no reason. You are my wife, the mother of my children. That's all that matters. I must be able to focus on my work, our work, not be constantly dealing with your hectoring and not to mention the personal attacks from your family. It has got to stop

Cimmie Yes it has Oswald.

My father has advised me to leave you.

Oswald What!

Cimmie He thinks you will never change and that my life will be a constant misery.

	I can go home, take the children.
Oswald	This is your home! Our home. Cimmie, please, you can't do this.
Cimmie	What choice have I got Oswald! You humiliate me!
Oswald	No, don't say that. I need you. You are my rock. I want us to bring up our children, together.
Cimmie	As good fascists?
Oswald	No. Yes. I want them to be proud of me. Of what I achieve. What we achieve together.
Cimmie	When you are an old man Oswald what will you look back on?

What will our children see in their father? What do you want to see in them? |
| Oswald | I will have saved the country that we love Cimmie. You know that. |
| Cimmie | I know you could do that.

But it won't be with me. Not unless you change.

(Pause) |
| Oswald | Let me hold Michael, please.

(He takes the child)

Perhaps he does look like me after all.

(Pause)

I *will*, change. I promise you. From now on, I'll tell you everything. |
| Cimmie | You'll tell me everything? And no more secret liaisons? |

Oswald	I want to share everything with you, my darling. No secrets.
Cimmie	How do you propose to do that?
Oswald	I'll confess my… failings. I'll write you a list. You will know the truth.
Cimmie	But no more….
Oswald	No more. You know I'm a man of honour. I'll keep my word.

(She takes the child back)

Cimmie	But Oswald….Please stop seeing Baba.

(She exits)

(Transition edited news reel moving from 1932 to 1933)

Scene 4 — BUF offices and barracks at The Black House, former College buildings, Chelsea — Tuesday 16 May 1933

(Projected image of the BUF Offices, Chelsea, with title of location and date - The BUF offices, Chelsea Tuesday 16 May 1933)

(Mosley, Jeffrey Hamm, and William Joyce, a BUF planning and action meeting. Jeffrey has several copies of The Greater Britain, which he passes to Oswald)

Jeffrey   Sign them, sir! They want that connection with you. But sign them Sir Oswald!

Oswald   Of course!

Joyce   Another two hundred members already this week. It's escalating. We can reach fifty thousand by Christmas.

Oswald   That's good, but I'm looking to five hundred thousand!

(Jeffrey and Joyce exchange glances)

Jeffrey   Both the Albert Hall and Olympia are booked.

Oswald   Good. We must have more stewards though. People like Kid Lewis can help. We need peer to peer advocacy to find the right people.

Joyce   He's Jewish. Kid Lewis is Jewish.

Oswald   That's of no consequence. He's a fighter. Bare fist fighter. He's got guts, and he's popular.

Joyce   Not with some of the Blackshirts.

Oswald   Now we have the barracks there is no reason to hold back on recruitment and training. Jeffrey let's get moving on this. There are lots of young men out there looking for a cause. Keep promoting how easy it is to join, all you need is a black shirt, just a shilling or two. People like the sense of belonging and we must reach the working man.

Joyce   Some of the members want more than a shirt. They want a proper uniform.

Jeffrey   Shall I look at options?

Joyce   I can do that.

Oswald   You're busy enough already, William. I need you to keep focus on the newspaper. If we can up the circulation then five hundred thousand members is possible. But we need distribution channels.

Joyce   The uniform would help that. Action has said it will provide one free to all those who sell an agreed number of copies. That's the route forwards.

Oswald   Full military uniform?

Joyce   Yes.

Oswald   I don't want anything elite.

Jeffrey   It's not elite, Sir. Joyce is right, it's responding to the membership.

Joyce   You agreed to keep out of the financial management of the party. Keep your nose clean. Leave us to make those decisions.

Oswald	Alright, if that's what you want. But the same rules of conduct must apply. The same codes whether you are in a black shirt or you have the full uniform.
	Action at meetings only when called for, by me, from the platform
	No violence to be initiated, only retaliatory
	No weapons
	Bare fists only
	No attacks on Jews
Jeffrey	We made that clear in the newspaper. Antisemitism is forbidden.
Oswald	Quite right.
Joyce	You'll need a uniform yourself, as The Leader.
Oswald	I suppose so.
Jeffrey	You'll look good. It will legitimise everything.
Joyce	You'll be the best dressed fascist in the world!
Oswald	What about the women?
Joyce	They will need one too.
Jeffrey	The Women's Section is growing faster.
Joyce	They love you, Oswald!
Oswald	Don't! I've got enough problems with women already.

(Diana enters and there is a pause as he passes her the flat keys. She exits)

> Cimmie's been throwing tantrums. Diana's very coy about it, fortunately.

Jeffrey   And Unity is pressing us to respond to her membership request.

Oswald   Absolutely not. She's a complete liability. Diana has no control over her sister. Going round Oxfordshire wearing a Nazi armband and goose stepping in front of local shopkeepers. She's a joke. Keep her away from me.

Joyce   She could bring publicity to the movement.

Oswald   The wrong sort. No, absolutely not. We are not German fascists. Supporters like Rothermere would be appalled.

          Then ditch them once the electorate give us their mandate. (Laughs)

          Gentlemen. We are on the way. Mass popularity is coming. Electoral success is round the corner. Let's focus on the creed. Put it on the back of every membership card.

          Opportunity shall be open to all

          Poverty shall be abolished

          The barriers of class shall be destroyed

Jeffrey   It all sounds terribly left wing.

Oswald   But the Labour Party didn't want to know. That is why we're here Jeffrey. And the creed, is why we will succeed.

(Enter Baba. She comes in uncertainly, wanting to speak to Mosley alone)

(Pause. They all look at her)

Oswald   Baba. Baba, what is it?

Baba   Cimmie….

	She's gone Oswald.
	She's gone.
Oswald	No! Baba, no.
	Oh my god.
Baba	I came straight here. She took a turn for the worse this morning. The doctor came again. There was nothing he could do. She was sinking fast.
Oswald	But last night….she was alright. I thought she looked better. That the worst was over.
Baba	Sorry. I'm sorry Oswald

(She hugs him/comforts him. Diana enters and stands watching)

Oswald	I betrayed her.
	What shall I do?
	Oh Cimmie. Forgive me.

(Mosley is unaware of Diana, but Baba gives her a deadly look. Mosley exits, followed by Baba)

Diana	What shall I do?
Jeffrey	Keep away, Diana. He will need time.
Joyce	We must protect the movement.
Jeffrey	Let him express his grief.
Joyce	But there is much work to do. That is what is important.
Diana	I know. I will support him in whatever way is necessary.

(Transition edited newsreel moving from 1933 to 1934)

Scene 5 — Lounge at the Dorchester Hotel, London — Saturday 6 Oct 1934

(Projected image of the interior of the Dorchester Lounge, with title of location and date - Lounge at the Dorchester Hotel, London — Saturday 6 Oct 1934)

(String quartet music playing quietly in the background)

(Diana is there first. Mosley enters. She sees him. He looks around and goes to kiss her on the lips).

Diana   Careful!

Oswald   I've missed you so much!

Diana   Rubbish. I'm sure you've been far too busy.

Oswald   My darling, it has seemed like an eternity.

Diana   But now I'm back. We can be together. Just the two of us. Couldn't we have met at Eaton Square? Or Ebury Street?

Oswald   I've hardly been in Belgravia. I can't remember what the flat looks like. I've been on the road, visiting party HQs all over the country, building support working towards the Hyde Park rally.

Diana   What's the point of me living round the corner if you don't come and visit me! (They sit)

Oswald   Don't let us quarrel Diana!

	I want to hear all about Germany. About Hitler and what he's doing.
Diana	He's wonderful Kit. So courteous and interesting. And the economic achievements! He must be hugely busy, but he was very welcoming to us. Unity is completely in thrall.
Oswald	And Nuremberg?
Diana	Just extraordinary. There must have been half a million people. They called it the Rally of Unity and Strength.
Oswald	Makes Hyde Park sound like a picnic.
Diana	Your movement will grow Kit. I am sure it will. You have the same oratorical power…. And you look so much better!
Oswald	But we're being boxed in. The BBC won't speak to me since Olympia. Lots of nonsense talked about the Black Shirts and our response to the intimidations. The press is ganging up and the violence has given Rothermere the jitters. His advertisers have put pressure on him.
Diana	Nothing can stop you.
Oswald	The BBC is winding up opposition and the establishment is battening down.
Diana	No such problem in Germany.
Oswald	Germany's different, Diana. We have to convince people by the merit of our arguments, not by using force.
Diana	But force is being used against you.

Oswald	I know. And there's pressure within the party to change policy. But I don't think the time is right. Not yet.
Diana	You're being called a thug, Kit. Maybe you need to be more thuggish!
Oswald	(squeezes her hand) Would you like that?
Diana	Rather!
	When are you going to come to Eaton Square and be thuggish with me?
Oswald	God, you are so attractive. I would take you there right now if I could!
	I'd take you here right now if I could

(Waiter approaches)

Waiter	Can I get you anything sir?
Oswald	Thank you. Tea for two, I think.
Waiter	Of course sir. (Pause) May I say, sir, how much I admire what you are doing?
Oswald	Thank you.
Waiter	We need change, sir. And you are just the man to make it happen.
Oswald	That's very kind.
Waiter	My friends and I. We're all going to join the Black Shirts. We're with you sir.
	We will fight for you sir.
Oswald	Not necessary, just at the moment! But thank you so much. Now, tea?
Waiter	Of course, sir.

Diana   You see. They love you.

              I love you. I adore you, Kit.

Oswald   Thank you my darling. It means everything. We will have some private time, soon. I promise you.

(Baba has entered and is looking around for Mosley)

              Oh damnation.

Diana   What?

(Oswald abruptly gets up and goes over to Baba)

Oswald   Baba, what are you doing here?

Baba   What are you doing here? With her? Jeffrey told me where you were. I thought we were seeing each other. I thought we were going to spend the afternoon together.

Oswald   We are. I will be at the flat at three, as promised.

(She goes to touch him)

              Careful.

Baba   Oswald, you're not playing games with me, are you? I couldn't bear that. It's bad enough that I have Cimmie on my conscience.

Oswald   Don't say that!

Baba   Sorry. I just can't bear seeing you with her.

Oswald   I have to. She's done so much for me. The contacts, the influence. You know that.

              Now go away, please. I can't wait to see you later. Touch you later.

Baba   Oh God. I'll be there, at three

Oswald   At three.

(Baba leaves. Oswald returns to Diana)

Diana   What did Baba want? Why didn't you bring her over?

Oswald   It was just about the children. She needed to let me know that Michael has not been well. She went to HQ. They told her I was here, with you, and wouldn't be coming back.

Diana   But I thought you needed to go back, that you were busy.

Oswald   I am, my darling. But I have got meetings elsewhere. Setting up events. You know how it is. It's very full-on at the moment.

Diana   Is Michael alright?

Oswald   Yes. Nothing serious. He misses his mother.

Diana   And the others?

Oswald   I've not seen enough of them lately. Too focused on Olympia, then Hyde Park. The party has got to take a strong step forward. We need another big jump in membership.

(Baba re-enters and comes over to the table)

Baba   I forgot to give you this (She kisses him full on the lips).

         I will see you later then.

(Diana stands)

Diana   How dare you.

(Diana sweeps the vase with the flower off the table)

Baba   Sit down Diana

(Diana steps towards Mosley and puts her hand on his shoulder)

Baba   Oh, now I see.

   Three o'clock then Oswald. Don't be late

(Baba leaves. The waiter sweeps up the mess and Diana speaks to him)

Diana   Thank you.
Waiter   Anything to help.
   (Pause)
Oswald   It's…not what it looks like Diana.
Diana   Really.
   So, are you going to see her?
Oswald   No. You're the one I care for.
   It's just that, she is so good with the children.
Oswald   Sit down. Please.
Diana   Marry me.
Oswald   What?
Diana   Marry me. You're free.
   I had planned to tell you…my divorce is through.
Oswald   I am so glad.
Diana   Let me help you. Properly. There will be more invitations to Germany. Unity is staying there.
Oswald   Do you know what they call her?
Diana   Who?

Oswald Baba

Baba Black Shirt. (They both laugh)

I like the fact you keep a distance. Are not at the rallies.

Diana   But you know I totally support you. In everything.

Oswald I know.

I will marry you. But not yet. It's too dangerous. For you. I don't want you to suffer abuse.

I just need to find the key. To stir the people, raise the bar. Move the membership forwards.

Diana   You could play the Jewish card.

Oswald What?

Diana   Hitler has united his country by identifying the enemy within. It's a conviction.

He is draining the swamp.

Oswald Now there's an idea.

(Transition edited news reel moving from 1934 to 1935)

6 - BUF Offices, January 1935

(Projected image of the outside of the BUF offices, with location and date - BUF Offices, January 1935)

(Baba and Jeffrey on stage. Baba is wearing her Black Shirt coat and trying on the military hat)

Baba   Jeffrey…how do I look?

Jeffrey   Charming, Mrs Metcalfe

Baba   Charming! I'm being serious. I want a real part in this movement.

Jeffrey   (Pause)

We'll have you fighting on the streets yet, Mrs Metcalfe.

Baba   Don't be silly. Just call me Baba. Everyone else does.

Jeffrey   I'm not sure that would be appropriate. Sir Oswald might…

Baba   Oh don't worry. I can manage him.

(Pause)

He is just a man you know.

Jeffrey   He's not just any man, Mrs Metcalfe.

(Curzon enters)

Lord Curzon, can I help you….

Curzon	Alexandra! You should not be here. I thought your husband had made the position clear.
Baba	My husband! No, don't leave Jeffrey. My father has nothing to say that can't be said in front of you.
Curzon	You must come home with me.
Baba	Who do you think you are?
Curzon	Think about your reputation!
	Can't you see? Mosley has attracted extremists to this organisation. I could never have imagined my daughter aligning herself to suffragettes.
Baba	Yes! The BUF supports women's rights! Do you really object to equal wages? To the right to effective birth control?
Curzon	Birth control?
Baba	That's correct isn't it Jeffrey?
Jeffrey	I believe so.
Curzon	Indoctrination.
Jeffrey	Now hold on...
Curzon	(To Jeffrey) Keep out of this.
	(To Baba) You look like a player in a costume drama!
Baba	I might say the same to you father. Aren't you forgetting that Cimmie was a founder member of this movement? She is still my role model.
Curzon	Cimmie was bewitched...by that man...as you are now.
Jeffrey	Pardon me, Lord Curzon...

Curzon	I thought I told you to stay out. Go and play soldiers somewhere else.
	This movement is a joke. A laughing stock. And it will soon be finished.
Jeffrey	I don't think so, Lord Curzon. The people are on side. The election will prove that.
Curzon	The people do not understand the realities of politics and the challenges of running this country. When the election comes circumstances will have changed. But, I'm not here to debate. I'm here on behalf of Rothermere. I had understood Mosley would be in the office today. Is he expected?
Jeffrey	Sir Oswald is lunching and will be arriving shortly...... in his own time.
Curzon	Lunching is he? Well I hope he has a good one, as what I have to say is likely to bring him indigestion.
Baba	You're enjoying this aren't you?
Curzon	Somewhat.
Jeffrey	Do you intend to wait?
Curzon	Yes…
	(Sits. Pause)
	and then Alexandra, you will come home with me.
	(Pause. Uncomfortable silence)

(Mosley enters with Diana, with a flourish. They are laughing, enjoying themselves.)

Oswald	Oh! Quite the family reunion.
Diana	(To Mosley) Do you want me to leave?

Baba   Yes. We all do.

Oswald   (To Diana) That will not be necessary. (Pause)

What have you come to say, Lord Curzon?

Curzon   I am here on behalf of Lord Rothermere. I'm instructed to give you this (passes over a formal legal document) and to inform you that all of his financial and public support for the BUF ceases as of this moment.

Furthermore, Lord Rothermere assures me that in future he will be taking a directly anti-British Union of Fascist stance in both the Daily Mail and the Daily Mirror.

We will see how that impacts on the popularity of your destructive movement.

So, what have you got to say?

Oswald   Well, well, well. So, the establishment has finally pressured Lord Rothermere into going against his better instincts.

No wonder this country is falling apart.

It only convinces me that we are heading more quickly towards the abyss.

Curzon   You should have stayed with the Tories Mosley. With your own kind. But you have too little patience don't you? In too much of a hurry. And now you're out of touch with the powers that be - only see things from your own limited perspective.

The future of this country is not just about you, Mosley, about your influence. The only person you lead now is yourself.

Oswald	….and when that abyss is reached, Lord Curzon, then the likes of you will find you have a very different future way of life.
Curzon	I doubt it.

What you say has repercussions, even if it is deluded. It influences people When will you learn that? You have created a howling mob that you can't control. All I can see in front of me now is a sad and flawed figure. |
Oswald	And all I see, now, is a broken man. A failure. That, I will never be!
Baba	Father….
Oswald	Tell Lord Rothermere we despise his cowardice. Fortunately, we have other new sources of finance to ensure the future of the British Union of Fascists.
Curzon	Alexandra. (Pause. Baba does not respond)

Then I'm sorry for you.

(Curzon walks out)

(Pause) |
| Jeffrey | Is that true Sir? That we can manage without the Daily Mail support? |
| Oswald | No.

(To Baba and Diana)

Leave me will you. I need to talk to Jeffrey.

(Pause. Neither woman wants to be the first to leave) |
| Diana | I'll be at Eaton Square when you've finished.

(To Baba) Charming uniform! |

(Baba walks out)

Rothermere will regret this (she leaves)

(Pause)

Oswald   You're right Jeffrey.

We will have to revisit our election planning. We cannot field candidates with reduced resources.

Finances are precarious and I cannot put in any more funds myself.

(Pause)

Don't say anything to the Executive though. Not yet.

(Pause)

You still believe in me Jeffrey.

Jeffrey   Of course sir. I will follow in whichever direction you go.. Even if that meant you were to rejoin the Labour Party.

Oswald   That is not an option.

But, thank you Jeffrey. We will find a way.

(Transition edited news reel moving from 1935 to 1936)

Scene 7 — Mosley's Private Gym, Savehay Farm, Denham — 30 September 1936

(Projected image of the gym with a large Union Jack, title with location and date – Mosley's Private Gym, Savehay Farm, Denham — 30 September 1936)

(Oswald is in a neutral space. It is a private den where he can go to shadow box, work out, and prepare his speeches. He has been working out, is red faced with effort, sweating)

(Oswald is shadow boxing whilst launching into a practice run of his speech)

Oswald   The people know that only the British Union of Fascists can address the challenges of our age. That is why you must vote for the BUF at the forthcoming election. (He has forgotten the next line of the speech and so repeats) That is why you must vote for the BUF at the forthcoming election.

(Jeffrey enters. Hangs back deferentially at first)

Oswald   The moment comes, and then you have to go over the top!

(Pause)

Come in Jeffrey.

Jeffrey   Sir, we have very clear intelligence. On Sunday there is going to be a massive gathering of Jews and communists, focused on Cable St.

	This could be the turning point. We think we should change policy and arm.
Oswald	We?
Jeffrey	Most of us. William Joyce in particular is pushing for action.
	We have to be ready. We must fight force with force, effectively. That means weapons, Sir. The time for gentlemen's rules has gone.
Oswald	Really.
Jeffrey	If we fight, then the people will come out with us. This could be the moment of change.
Oswald	What are you suggesting?
Jeffrey	Some of us think it is now or never. We're not going to change politics passively. We have to take the initiative. Look at what has happened in Germany. A populist uprising. Storm Parliament if necessary. It's the moment.
Oswald	It won't work. Not at this time.
	The economic crisis has to peak first. And then force may not even be necessary.
	If we use force now then we will be crucified in the press. You must tell Joyce and the others to stand down. We must not change path.
Jeffrey	They may not listen to you.
Oswald	Are you listening to me? Is this insurrection?
Jeffrey	I am just trying to share the mood. The position. The fact we're going to be in a big bloody fight on Sunday.

Oswald   I relish a fight. You know that. When do we not have a fight?

Jeffrey   This is going to be different. It might be the moment!

Oswald.   No. You're wrong. I will know when the moment comes. And when I am on that platform, when I call on the black shirts to act, they act, but not before, and not with arms. We must maintain discipline.

Jeffrey   I'll see what I can do.

Oswald   Leave me. I have a speech to prepare.

Jeffrey   (He gives the fascist salute) Perish Judah.

Oswald   Perish Judah. Is that the way forwards? Is that the way to build the membership? Does the end justify the means? The goal has to be real change. We must sweep away these dull, politicians who lack courage and determination. I can change this country. I can make Britain great again. Who else will do it? I will build a legacy that history will remember.

(He reverts to his speech)

Our plans are no less than the complete reform of the Parliamentary system, a draining of the swamp, and with the removal of the regulations and control that are a barrier to action.

Let us once again hold high the head of Great Britain. Let us lift strongly the voice of Empire.

This British flag still challenges the winds of destiny. This flame still burns. The time has come and for us… it is Britain first!

(During the above, Baba, Joyce and Jeffrey enter and join him on the podium. Oswald dons his BUF hat)

Scene 8 — The Battle of Cable St — Sunday 4 October 1936

(Projection of moving image of the crowd, with sound, plus title with location and date The Battle of Cable St — Sunday 4 October 1936)

(Mosley, with Joyce, Jeffrey, and Baba)

(Raised voices over the noise of the crowd)

Joyce   What did I tell you? There are barricades across Cable St, and a huge crowd behind. We need to attack, force our way through. Smash the Jews.

Oswald No! Let the police clear the way. It is their job. We have a right to parade where we want. Their responsibility is to clear the route.

Joyce   So, you're just going to stand here and wait.

Oswald Parade here and wait. Show our discipline.

Joyce   I thought you were the man of action!

Oswald Are you calling me a coward!

        I fought in the trenches, William. I flew a biplane over German lines.

Joyce   Well act then. Show us the way.

Oswald When will you learn strategy! You want to get your head broken for no better reason than to cuff a few Jews! Our strength is our ability to show discipline.

We stay here!

Joyce   And lose the fight. (Joyce exits)

Oswald   But win the war!!

(Mosley climbs onto a small podium. This can be a box to mask the floor mounted projector)

Oswald   My friends. The Jews and the communists have erected barricades and blocked the streets, denying us access through Cable St. Once that route has been cleared, we *will* march through. We will march and only retaliate, when attacked, and then you can respond like for like, but we march on. We do not lose our discipline. We march on to Victoria Park and there I will speak in full to the assembled crowd. WE WILL BE HEARD.

(Enter Actor 4 as a senior police officer who addresses Mosley)

Police   Can you come down a minute please sir?

Oswald   Are we ready to move on?

Police   No.

Oswald   When will you have cleared the way.

Police   We are not clearing the way, sir. You need to turn back.

Oswald   No. It is your duty to enable us to march down that street, and all the way to Victoria Park. You have to clear the way.

Police   Not any more sir. I have my instructions. From the Home Secretary.

We attempted to move the barricades but the resistance was too strong. My officers were at severe risk. I have spoken to the Commander who has been in touch with the Home Secretary. My orders are to tell you to turn round and address your supporters in Hyde Park. Then to disperse peacefully and quickly. You will not be marching through Cable St today.

(Mosley climbs back onto the podium. Through the following speech there is a constant hubbub, cheering and applause, chanting, as well as moments of serious heckling and disturbance)

Oswald   Once again we are being denied our right to free expression!

The Establishment, bullied by the Jewish financiers, has backed down. The Home Secretary personally authorised our march, but now, faced by the failure of the police to remove the protesters and barricades, he has backed down.

(Louder heckling and disturbance)

You see, once again we are being shouted down.

My voice will be heard.

Yes, you see them…over there. The Jews. I call on our honourable stewards, our black shirt friends to deal with them. Remove them.

(Disturbance noise, clearly with violence involved, continues intermittently, building to a crescendo of Perish Judah chants at the end of Mosley's speech) at which point he cannot be heard. Mosley is getting angry, losing control)

They said "You shalt not pass!" I tell them "We shall pass. We will fight the Jewish agitators that attempt to prevent a democratic right to freedom of speech. We are coming for them every night of the week and we will rid East London of these…

(Group chanting of Perish Judah. Actors, except Mosley join in chanting and lift their arms in the fascist salute. Mosley does not join in and is chanted out. He continues speaking for a few moments but cannot be heard at all)

(Blackout)

INTERVAL

Scene 9 — Joseph Goebbels' House — Tuesday 6 October 1936

(Projected image of the guest bedroom in Joseph Goebbel's house, Berlin, plus title location and date - Oswald and Diana's wedding night, Joseph Goebbels' House — Tuesday 6 October 1936)

(Music underplaying the scene as if the radio from a distance – I only have Eyes for You, Ben Selvin's Knickerbockers, or alternative soft 30's tune)

Diana   Kit. You're in such a strange mood.

Oswald Sorry.

Diana   It is our wedding night!

Oswald I touched on the funding issue, with Adolf. He seemed disinterested.

Diana   His command of English is not good.

Oswald It wasn't that. The translator was there. He avoided the subject. Just kept reverting to his plans for Czechoslovakia.

Diana   Kit, tonight, this moment, these few days…are really special to me.

(Diana puts her arms round Oswald)

Oswald I think there is going to be a war, Diana.

Diana   No. Adolf doesn't want a war.

Oswald I'm sorry. It's just…it brings it all back.

After the last one, I promised myself, that we must not have another war. It's what drove me into politics.

Diana   I know.

Oswald You can't imagine what I'd seen, in the air corps, and in the trenches; the indifference of the machine guns, the anonymity of it. Mud and blood. The brutal waste of young men. Men of all classes. Working men with sweethearts at home. Young British officers, beautiful, honed, fit, with all their potential, and not involved in some frolic of a ballroom skirmish, but in total obliteration. The cowardice of gas. God.

Then afterwards those appalling celebrations. Trafalgar Square. I saw people, crowds of them, who had never fought, never experienced the reality, dancing, singing, cheering, as if we should all be joyful, forgetting the thousands who were blown apart on the battlefields of France and Belgium.

Diana   But you can stop it my darling.

You can stop the warmongers.

Keep speaking out, building the movement. You will prevail.

Oswald We're being shackled. My voice is stifled. They're bringing in a new Public Order Act, banning the wearing of uniform, at least at outdoor rallies. We

	won't be able to steward our own meetings. It is a personal attack.
Diana	Don't think about it tonight. Let tonight just be about us. Leave the politics behind, just for once.
	(Pause)
	I know you are striving for a better world, Kit, a peaceful world. You are the leader who can make that happen. I have total faith in you.

(They move to kiss, but the music stops abruptly and we hear Hitler delivering an impassioned speech on the radio. The volume is turned up and his voice is invasive. It breaks the romantic spell. Diana and Oswald break apart. They are frustrated at first, but then burst into laughter)

Oswald	I'm not like Hitler, am I?
Diana	Of course not!
Oswald	Chaplin does such a perfect impersonation.
Diana	Adolf is so clever. So charming. But all the Nazis are so terribly ugly!
	(Pause. They listen)
Oswald	The power of radio. If only I had that option.
Diana	Why not?
Oswald	You know why not.
Diana	We could get our own license.
Oswald	Be realistic, Diana, the BBC has a monopoly.
Diana	Well, get a German license. It would still reach the south east of England.

	The movement needs funds. If Hitler will not support directly, ask him for a German radio license.
Oswald	You know I think that is rather brilliant.
Diana	A voice, and advertising revenue.
	(The speech on the radio stops abruptly)
Oswald	I don't think Goebbels likes me though.
Diana	Hitler wanted us here. The little man is jealous of your looks. (Sharply) You've not approached Magda, have you? Don't tell me…
Oswald	You silly Nardy. Don't be jealous. I have married you, haven't I?
Diana	So you have. Aren't we awful? When we're here enjoying their hospitality.
	(Music is playing, quietly once again – Maria Leeser, or alternative 30's tune)
Oswald	Goebbels will have a say – about a radio license.
Diana	I can help.
Oswald	Well, Adolf seems to trust you.
Diana	He's invited Unity to Berchtesgaden.
	There may be an opportunity.
Oswald	Be careful.
	A radio license could be our salvation. Mussolini's support for us is wavering, and he's about to sign a protocol with Hitler. Fascist parties of Europe coming together.
	We have to fight to avoid war.

	The radio license is brilliant. Will you speak to Adolf?
Diana	Of course.
Oswald	Thank you. For everything. (Pause)
	Look at you. Gorgeous, intelligent, and so desirable. That come to bed look.
Diana	Then what are we waiting for?

(They kiss and exit together hand in hand)

Scene 10 — BUF offices at Stanhope Gardens, Kensington — February 1937

(Projected image of the offices of the BUF. There is a squalor to the office and the mood is downbeat compared to the previous BUF office scene. Plus, title with location and date - BUF offices at Stanhope Gardens, Kensington — February 1937)

(Joyce is in the office, Mosley enters)

Joyce   Perish Judah!

(He gives the fascist salute to Mosley)

But now we can't even turn up in uniform to manage the meetings.

The people of this country are in tune with anti-Jewish sentiments. We need to play that to its full advantage.

Oswald   My only concern is to stop the Jewish minority from taking us into a war with Germany.

Joyce   You are out of touch with the membership.

Oswald   That membership was declining until I focused on the anti-war pitch.

We lost it after Cable St. The Establishment and the press have undermined us.

Joyce   Because we didn't take the momentum when the opportunity was there.

Oswald   Are you attacking my leadership?

Joyce   I'm just saying that we need to be strong in reasserting who we are to galvanise wide public support.

Oswald   So, we agree. But it's about responding to the fear of war. That is the key issue, William. We must not succumb to the warmongers. It would mean total destruction.

          Our anti-war focus will reassert our position. You'll see the effect of that in these local election results. We are on the way back. We can succeed.

Joyce   But if the worst happens?

Oswald   War with Germany?

Joyce   Yes. How would you instruct the membership? What should we do?

(Enter Jeffrey Hamm with newspaper)

Oswald   I will encourage our members to volunteer and fight. But that will not be necessary.

Joyce   I see.

Jeffrey   Don't be too optimistic Oswald. I am sorry to bring bad news.

          First announcements of the Municipal Election results.

          Labour, 450,000 votes, 75 seats

          Conservatives 378,000 votes, 49 seats

          BUF......15,278 votes. No seats

(Pause)

Joyce   We're on the way back, are we?

Jeffrey   Shut it, William.

(Pause)

Jeffrey   Maybe you should have stayed with the Labour Party, Oswald.

Oswald   Too little patience.

(Pause)

Too little patience.

(Pause)

Oswald   We need to get the executive together. There are decisions to be made.

(Pause)

I need to make decisions.

But we still have a lot of popular support… whatever the election results suggest.

We are not finished yet.

Scene 11 — Dorchester Hotel Lounge — 30 April 1937

(Projected image of interior of the Dorchester lounge. Plus, title with location and date- Dorchester Hotel Lounge — 30 April 1937)

(String quartet music playing quietly in the background. The waiter is a presence on and off through the scene)

(Diana is already at a table. Baba enters and comes over to her)

Baba	I thought I would find you here.
	Quite a regular haunt, isn't it?
Diana	Sit down. Have some tea.
Baba	No thank you (she sits anyway)
	So, you are married.
	(Pause)
Diana	Yes.
Baba	Did you think you could keep it a secret?
Diana	We've told no one. Oswald preferred it that way.
Baba	I bet he did. He has still been seeing me you know.
Diana	I don't believe you.
	(Pause)

	How did you find out?
Baba	Your brother told me.
Diana	What?!
Baba	He thinks Oswald is a cad. Those were his words.
Diana	Bit old fashioned. That does not sound like my brother.
Baba	Oh I can assure you it was. He seemed to think you were afraid of it becoming public.
Diana	I'm not afraid! It's Oswald.
	He thinks that I might be vulnerable if the marriage is made public.
Baba	Does he?
Diana	Personally, I don't give a damn. As far as I'm concerned, all that matters is that he's mine.
Baba	You really think so?
Diana	I do.
Baba	There's more to vulnerability than physical risk.
Diana	What are you implying?
Baba	Do you think this will do his reputation any good? His political career? Being married to one of the Mitford's. A woman who spends half her life in Nazi Germany and whose sister is practically in bed with the Fuhrer!
Diana	Do you want to know why I spend so much time in Germany?
Baba	Go on. Surprise me.
Diana	I think I might.

I've been negotiating, on Oswald's behalf, for a German radio license, so we can transmit to south east England, so that the party can benefit from advertising revenue, the party that you purport to support.

(Joyce enters and speaks to the waiter. The waiter waits for acknowledgement from Diana before indicating Joyce can approach the table)

Baba   That is very interesting. But I am no longer a party member. I have torn up my membership card. The values of the BUF are no longer in accord with my thinking.

Diana   You mean since my husband dropped you?

Baba   Has he? No, since the values changed and I felt that Cimmie would no longer have approved. If Cimmie was still here, she would not have let Oswald go down this path.

Diana   I think you overrate all of our influence. Especially your own.

(Joyce approaches the table)

Joyce   Lady Mosley. Can I have a word?

Baba   Lady Mosley! So, they know about it too.

(To Joyce) You kept that very quiet, didn't you?

Joyce   Not my secret to tell, Mrs Metcalfe.

Diana   What do you want Mr. Joyce?

Joyce   Well, you are the power behind the throne. Everyone knows that.

Baba   The power behind the throne!

Diana   Not true. Oswald does exactly what he wants to do.

Joyce   The man of action.

Baba   He certainly does what he wants.

Diana   I don't think I can help you.

Joyce.   I think you can. You must.

   He's decimating the party.

Baba   You mean he's getting rid of you!

Joyce   We should have been breaking the barricades and storming Parliament, not in fighting, sacking the members.

Diana   He is The Leader. Any decisions are his.

Joyce   He's losing his nerve. You're strong. You could make him see sense.

Baba   She could?

Diana   Can I ask you something, Mr Joyce, something that has always intrigued me?

Joyce   Of course

Diana   How did you get that hideous scar?

(Baba laughs)

Joyce   It doesn't help me look pretty does it.

   A communist razor blade, 1932. That is why I have no truck with the bare fists nonsense. Still, that's the aristocracy for you.

Diana	My husband has a vision, and he will not be derailed. If he sees the need to let some of you go, then he will have good reasons.
Joyce	It's not just some, Lady Mosley, its three quarters of the paid staff.
	If this is implemented, we will have no alternative but to initiate a rival party.
Diana	And how do you propose to do that?
Joyce	We will mobilize the people. We will focus even more on the Jewish threat.
Diana	You will simply use hate.
Joyce	The people know what is the cause of their disempowerment. By attacking the Jews, we will take back control. We won't let Cable St happen again, standing there, as if on a parade, doing nothing.
Diana	The press called it the Battle of Cable Street!
Baba	You don't have the organizational skill to set up something new.
Joyce	Really!
	I wouldn't have allowed the Public Order Act to *stop us* wearing the uniform.
	Tell your husband, there will be a vote of confidence. Talk to him, before it's too late. He has to reinstate those he has fired. Otherwise, I can't answer for what will happen.
Diana	Is that a threat, Mr Joyce?
Joyce	Your friend Hitler will despise him.

Diana	Hitler knows better. And Hitler would probably have had *you* shot.
Joyce	I doubt it. If there is a war with Germany, I know where I will be, in Berlin, alongside your sister, whilst Sir Oswald will probably be in prison.
Diana	Unity has threatened to shoot herself if there's a war. Perhaps you should do the same.
Joyce	No! I will fight with the Germans. Your husband will have lost the opportunity to run this country under a German occupation.
Diana	My husband would never do that.. But maybe I should put in a word for you with Mr Hitler.
Joyce	Is that a threat, Lady Mosley?
Baba	It has been fascinating listening to this, but I must go.
	I can't wait to share the news about your German radio license. Very loyal.
Diana	It will soon be public anyway
Baba	The marriage or the license?
Diana	Both.
	It will have to be. We shall start broadcasting.
	Pity you will miss the opportunity to be part of that Mr Joyce.
	(Joyce exits)
	And as far as the marriage goes…I'm pregnant, so you see it can't be a secret for much longer.

(Transition edited news reel moving from 1937 to 1941)

Scene 12 — Holloway Prison — 24 December 1941

(Projected image of a prison cell at Holloway, plus title with location and date - Holloway Prison — 24 December 1941)

(Diana and Mosley are allowed to live together, albeit in Holloway prison, for the first time since May 1940)

(Diana is wrapped in a blanket. Oswald enters, escorted by the prison officer. Oswald is wearing a heavy great coat and scarf. He looks around the prison cell)

Oswald   Diana.

(They look at each other. She comes to him)

Diana   Welcome home, Kit. Such as it is.

(They embrace and kiss, both overcome)

Oswald   I didn't think this reunion would happen.

Diana   It was my brother. He went to see Winston, who feels guilty, apparently. He said our imprisonment was an outrage.

    At least now we can be together. I hope Holloway is better than Brixton!

Oswald   You…look…amazing.

Diana   No lipstick, no make-up I'm afraid. But at least now we have each other. This will be the happiest Christmas of my life.

Oswald   (looking round). Here in our suite. Our Holloway suite.

Diana   Darling, we have a garden! Well, a patch of sooty ground. I'm sure we will be able to at least grow fraise des bois.

Oswald   Oh for a strawberry!

(Pause)

We will farm my love… on a mini scale! And we'll cook for the children when they come to see us.

(Diana is unable to speak)

Oswald   I know. I know. Alex is finding it very hard.

Diana   Kit, it's unbearable. He cries so much when it is time to leave. He grabs hold of me and won't let go. He has to be wrenched away. How long is this going to go on?

Oswald   Have you been to Ascot?

Diana   Yes.

I didn't tell you because it was too negative. The Committee was hostile. They suggested I had convinced Adolf that Britain would never fight.

Oswald   It was a whitewash, like mine. They kept asking me about antisemitism. I don't know why I did this, but I told them my grandfather led the House of Commons opposition to Jewish emancipation, and that maybe it runs in the family. I could not take it seriously.

	I never thought I would go to Ascot for anything other than the races.
	You know we are virtually the only ones left inside. Apart from us there's Jeffrey, brought back from the Falklands, where apparently, he might have been dangerous. Oh, and that poor BUF beekeeper. He made the mistake of writing in his diary, "Remove the Queen and replace with an Italian."
Diana	You look thin. You're not well.
Oswald	But all the better now, for being with you, my darling. (He breaks down)
Diana	What's happened?
	(Pause)
Oswald	They have taken Nick and Michael away.
	My former sister-in-law, I cannot say her name, has obtained the right to determine their education and future.
	I am through with them, the whole damn Curzon family.
Diana	You will get them back…when this is over. Baba will not win.
Oswald	Will it ever be over?

(Cecil Syers has entered unobtrusively. The prison officer stands in the background until Syers introduces himself)

Syers	I think it will, Sir Oswald. Winston is very determined.

	Cecil Syers (he offers his hand to each in turn. He is aware of how cold her hand is).
	I'm Winston's Private Secretary. He asked me to come and see you both.
Diana	Is this to initiate our release?
Cecil	I'm afraid not.
Diana	I was breast feeding when I was taken from Max and brought here. My baby was four weeks old.
Cecil	I know.
Diana	I was told I would be held for the weekend. It has been eighteen months.
Cecil	I am very sorry. Winston is very sorry. He is, however, hamstrung. Mr Attlee….
Oswald	Attlee!
	(Pause)
Cecil	Winston told me that he had known *you* as a child, Lady Mosley.
Diana	I see. So why are you here?
Cecil	Winston is aware that circumstances have been difficult for you both. I am enabled to make some arrangements to improve things. Hence the new internment provisions (indicating them together).
Diana	Improve things how?
Cecil	Well, bathing arrangements for instance.
Diana	Bathing arrangements!
	Are you aware of the conditions here Mr Syers?
Cecil	I am seeing them now, at first hand.

Diana   The women here are locked in our cells in the dark, during blackout, for up to fifteen hours. I hear distressed women crying out and calling for help. Some are poor working women from the East End. Sex workers. Others are refugees who fled the country you and your colleagues have decided is the enemy. One of my fellow inmates, a German dissident, managed to reach England on a small boat having spent time in Dachau concentration camp, which she assures me is more hospitable than Holloway. When that small boat landed on the beach, she was immediately seized and detained.

Oswald   And yet this country is apparently fighting for liberty.

Diana   But, Mr Syers, you were about to offer improved bathing facilities.

Do you mean for everyone?

Cecil   No, just for you.

Diana   Thank you, but no. I cannot justify having privileges that you will not offer to the other women with whom I share this detention.

Oswald   Please give Winston our regards, and remind him that many members of my former party, now banned, are currently in the armed forces serving our country. I always stated that in the event of war our members would loyally support Great Britain. We are not traitors.

Cecil   Pardon me, but Lady Mosley did have a number of meetings with Adolf Hitler.

Oswald	So did Neville Chamberlain and many of your civil service colleagues. Have they also been imprisoned?
Cecil	Winston's view is that you are *safer* in prison. If you were released, you would be at the mercy of the mob.
Oswald	What you mean is that the so-called mob still supports us.
	Thank you, Mr Syers. I am sure we will manage very well with the bathing arrangements that are currently in place.
Cecil	So be it.
	It's difficult to know what to do with a man like you, Sir Oswald.

(Syers exits. Silence for a moment or two)

Oswald	The mercy of the mob!
Diana	We have each other still. We *are* together. Poor Kit, you need to recover your health. After the war is over, perhaps you should……
	The movement is dead. We must accept that.
Oswald	The movement is dead?
	(Pause)
	The movement is dead! That movement. I need to reflect, to read. There will be a new vision.
	(Pause)
	This country needs it. I am not done yet. My moment *will* come.
Diana	What will you be like as an old man, Kit!

(Diana removes Oswald's prison coat, revealing jacket and bow tie underneath as in scene 1)

(Diana exits)

Oswald   It's the fire inside.

(Transition edited news reel moving from 1941 back to 1961)

Scene 13 — Anniversary celebration — Friday 6 October 1961, midnight

(Projected image of the house at Orsay as for the Prologue, plus title with location and date - Anniversary celebration — Friday 6 October 1961, midnight)

(Music playing – Cheek to Cheek, Fred Astaire)

Oswald   It's the fire inside, just as I remember it!

(Diana enters)

Oswald   I feel like dancing (he goes to take her hand)

Diana   I'm tired Kit

Oswald   I wish you would stop calling me that.

Diana   What?

Oswald   Reminds me too much of the old days.

Diana   What has brought this on?

Oswald   I'm on fire

Diana   You are drunk

Oswald   I'm looking forwards Diana

   I can see the future.

   We can sweep all these buffoons away – McMillan, Gaitskell, Wilson for God's sake.

They have destroyed an Empire and the British economy is sinking like a stone.

The moment is close.

Diana   You've been saying that for a long time my darling.

Oswald   You are not losing faith, not now!

Diana   Of course not.

You will turn things round. I can see that. Europe is the answer.

Oswald   Exactly. It is a bold new vision. It's radical. Who would have thought it possible, after Nuremberg.

Time marches on.

I just have to deal with the idiots who are still misguided by racial hatred.

Do you know what Grundy said earlier? "The problem isn't the Blacks it's the Jews, and if you're looking for the first man in Britain to turn on the gas taps, I'm here!"

Where do these people come from? It's a confederacy of dunces. I must go back and stop this nonsense.

Diana   You attract them, Oswald. You always have. You just have to accept that.

Oswald   No!

This is far too important. I offer a vision, a European vision that will change the whole direction of Western Europe. Imagine, in sixty years' time, a Europe united with a common economic plan, a shared currency and a governance that operates across the continent.

Diana   It's wonderful.

Oswald It's more than wonderful. And within that there will be a means for freedom of speech. My successors will be able to speak widely, to everyone. Mass communication will be available and there will be no more censorship by default. Just think what that will mean. What it would have meant back in the thirties. Men of talent will be able to emerge.

Diana   Or women.

Oswald Of course, Diana, of course.

True leaders will be enabled, and they will build popular support. The will of the people, through populism, will finally prevail.

Diana   You must make it happen.

Oswald I will. The fire is there.

The sleeping giant is alive again. Now let's have that dance.

(They start to waltz. As they dance Diana becomes increasingly uneasy)

Diana   I can't do this Oswald. (She breaks the dance)

Oswald What's the matter?

Diana   The trouble is I recognise your mood.

(The music ends and the needle is left scratching at the end of the record)

Oswald What do you mean. The world is ours Diana. We can make things happen again. Make things happen, not hang our heads in shame like David and Wallis. They have no guts, no drive.

Diana   But your drive, Oswald that is what I recognise. That particular drive. So charming, so personable.

    It has always been the same.

Oswald   What do you mean.

Diana   When you are in love. When you're in pursuit. I have seen it too many times.

    Who is it this time Oswald? Tell me. I have a right to know.

    I will not be betrayed again.

Oswald   How can you say this! You have always been the special one, Diana.

    You know that!

Diana   Have I? Have I really?

    What about Baba?

    I never knew whether you slept with her after we were married.

    Why can't you be honest for once? Tell me who it is.

Oswald   There's no-one. It's all in your imagination.

    The worst moments of my life have been when I've been away from you.

Diana   You mean when you were in Brixton?

    (Pause)

Oswald   Not just then.

Diana   This life has not been easy you know.

Oswald   I know.

No regrets Diana, no looking back. Not now. There is so much potential, so much to achieve.

(Pause)

(He kisses her, thinks the moment has passed) Thank you for everything my darling. I know you've put up with a lot.

Diana   I have.

(Pause)

So, who is it?

Oswald   There is nobody, Nardy. I promise you.

(Pause)

Earlier, during the reception. I was on my own for a few minutes.

I thought I saw Cimmie. Someone who looked like Cimmie, perhaps. I don't know.

(Pause)

That's all.

(Pause)

Diana   That's even worse, Oswald.

And it's our wedding anniversary.

Twenty-five years ago, *today*.

(She walks out)

Scene 14 — Rediffusion Television Studio — Wednesday 15 November 1967

(Projected image of a 1960's TV studio, plus title with location, and date - Rediffusion Television Studio — Wednesday 15 November 1967)

(Programme music for The Frost Report overlays entrance of Frost and Mosley. Actors 2, 3 and 4 sit in the audience as if members of the TV studio audience)

Frost   Hello, good evening and welcome. Tonight, the subject of The Frost Report is Sir Oswald Mosley.

Brilliant economist, at one time possible future Prime Minister, a man of wit and charm, but also a man with an association with East End riots, British fascism and antisemitism. This is his first appearance on British television.

Sir Oswald. First of all, what have you got to say about that antisemitic accusation?

Oswald I am very happy to answer that. I have nothing against anybody born a Jew. From the beginning of my movement in 1932 until 1934, antisemitism was never once mentioned. Then our meetings started to be disrupted by communists and Jews. I thought the Jews wanted a war with Germany, because of the persecution there. I was totally

	opposed to any such war and that was the beginning of the quarrel.
Frost	Your supporters attacked Jewish people. Why did you condone that violence?
Oswald	I can tell you exactly, and provide evidence if necessary. It was in self-defence. When you are attacked, you have to fight back. We explicitly told our members *not* to initiate violence. Anybody we found attacking Jews was expelled from our movement.

(Interruptions from the audience – played by the other actors - overlaid, Mosley trying to speak over the top)

Actor 5:	How can you say that when your Black Shirts were kicking Jews at your own meetings.
Actor 3:	You were a friend of Hitler's. You can't be more anti- Semitic than that.
Actor 2:	You met with Hitler. There's pictures of you with fascist leaders. You were all anti-Semitic.
Oswald	That is quite untrue. I was never a friend of Hitler. I admired his economic achievements. You won't let me speak. This is what it's like.
Frost	Let him answer the accusation. Let me ask you… if Hitler had survived at the end of the war would you have been in favour of him being tried and convicted for war crimes?
Oswald	Yes. I think anyone who has committed crimes should always be tried. The murder of the Jews in the concentration camps was an outrageous and vile crime.

Frost   But many would argue that your quarrel with the Jews, as you put it, condoned the Nazi treatment of that minority. You are a dangerous man. Is that not the case?

(Applause from studio audience)

Oswald   If we engaged in war with every country where a minority is persecuted, we should never be out of conflict. I claimed the liberty….

(Further interruptions from the audience, overlaid and played by the other actors)

Actor 3:   Your members were always looking for a fight.

Actor 5:   You were beating up people on the streets. Marching through areas where Jewish people lived, just to provoke them.

Actor 2:   You ignored the persecution of Jews. Why don't you admit it?

Oswald   I claimed the liberty…(more shouts over his voice). I claimed…they won't let me speak.

Frost   Let him speak. You're proving..

Oswald   They're proving my case, up to the hilt. I claimed the liberty to persuade the British people by my voice, if I could, to make peace in 1939. I claimed that liberty, and it was denied me by putting me in jail to stop me making speeches.

Frost   You say, absolutely definitively, that anybody who was guilty of antisemitism was expelled from your party. How can you possibly expect people to believe it, when everybody who watched the events of the 1930's associates your party totally

	with racial hatred and antisemitism. Either what you are saying is not true, or you were the most ineffectual, put-upon, unable to impose his leadership on a party, party leader that has ever been seen.

(Applause from studio audience)

Oswald	We were in a fight. We were fighting Jews for one reason, to stop a war with Germany.
Frost	But Sir Oswald, your movement had already failed. And today you've nothing to show for it. Most recently your Union Movement candidates stood in elections in 66 and chose three areas where they could capitalise most on racial unrest, polling just over 3% of the votes. There's nothing left to show from your movement is there? What went wrong?
Oswald	That again is quite untrue. There is no racial problem in Shoreditch where I stood.
Frost	3%
Oswald	I polled 4.8% not 3%
Frost	You 4.8%. A colleague of yours 4.6% and another 2.9%
Oswald	We averaged 3.7%
Frost	That's what I said.

(Laughter from studio audience)

Oswald	And if you must talk so much about Hitler, who doesn't actually interest me very much – last year we polled just about double what he did five years

	before he came into power. So don't be too cocky about that!!
Frost	Do you think democracy is right for Britain today?
Oswald	Parliamentary control must be maintained – subject to the right of government to act.
Frost	And do you think one day you will still get power?
Oswald	Well, there are two ways of getting power…one is by a consensus of the nation.
	(Pause)
Frost	And the other….?
Oswald	Is to build up a committed and forceful grass roots movement of the people.
Frost	So, ultimately you *would* storm Parliament.
Oswald	In life always try to do things gently, and only get tough when you have to get tough.
Frost	Alright. So with Sir Oswald Mosley's message – In life always try to do things gently, we'll say good night.
	(Frost Report music plays out)

Scene 15 — Another Anniversary, Oswald Mosley's Study at Orsay — Thursday 6 October 1976

(Projected image of Mosley's study – rather traditional, upper class, Edwardian style furniture and décor, plus title with location and date- Oswald Mosley's Study at Orsay — Thursday 6 October 1976)

(We see Oswald sunk in his thoughts. A telephone has been placed on the table beside him. The audio we hear in the scene are Oswald's thoughts inside his head, a recording of his voice)

Oswald   Another anniversary.

           Ruby no less.

           Waiting for fate to decide the future.

           Old and celibate.

Audio   *The opposite of my childhood fantasy. Imagining, dreaming, living, a secret room full of young girls. The harem of the great leader. There to do my bidding, and pleased to do it. Pure pleasure and excitement.*

Oswald   That is what I need now, before it's too late. The spark to ignite passion in readiness for the call.

           And if the call does not come, will I have failed? No! Don't use that word.

	And meanwhile what a compromise. Being allowed into Europe. How patronizing. They should have listened to my vision, to the Venice Conference.
	Still, the call may come. And I must be ready when it comes. Have the fire again. The fire inside to fight the doubters, the hecklers. Am I a dangerous man?
Audio	*Israel was just what I proposed. My plan. And the Jews have a voice now. But still the lies about the war are perpetuated.*
	(Telephone rings. Oswald allows it to ring for some time, almost afraid to answer)
Oswald	So, this is it. The call, at last. The moment of truth.
	(He picks up the receiver)
	Hallo.
	Yes.
	Uhuh.
	(Pause)
	I see. How long?
	I said, how long?
	(Pause)
	I see.
	That makes everything very clear.
	(Pause)
	Thank you.
	(Pause)

	Right. Goodbye.
Audio	*That recurring dream. In the House of Commons, speaking for hours, without notes. The silence of members moved to a rapturous intensity of concentration, knowing the truth of what is being spoken. Then coming out of the reverie, exhausted, looking round. And the benches are empty. There is no one there.*
	(Pause)
Oswald	So, that is it then. Parkinson's disease they tell me. Two to three years at most
	(He replaces the receiver fully on the cradle)
	What will be my legacy?
Audio	*The world will wake up. The time for strong leaders will come. Popular leaders who say what they think and carry it through*
	I will be their inspiration.
Oswald	My Vision will be fulfilled by them..

Oswald exits. Optional short edited moving image of Diana Mosley)

Scene 16 — A small apartment, Christchurch, New Zealand — Wednesday 6 March 2019

(Projected image cuts to a dingy, small apartment, plus title with location and date - A small apartment, Christchurch, New Zealand — Wednesday 6 March 2019)

(Brenton Tarrant enters with chair, tripod and mobile phone. He is listening to a recording on the phone as he sets up the tripod downstage centre. The audience can hear the audio)

(Recording of Trump as if from phone – "We are going to Washington DC and we are going to drain the swamp." Group chants of "Drain the Swamp")

(Tarrant adjusts the phone to video mode and then sits staring at the phone camera on the tripod. He is sitting astride a chair with his arms folded on its back. Confident, relaxed, excited. He begins recording his "message")

Tarrant   6 March 2019. This is a week the world will remember.

         I am Brenton Tarrant. I am an Eco-Fascist.

         This is My Manifesto – The Great Replacement.

         Today I will check out the Al-Noor Mosque in Christchurch during their Friday Prayers.

Next Friday I will carry out an attack against the invaders, and will live stream the attack through Facebook.

I have seen what is happening in Europe. I am with my Serbian brothers.

My action is a pre-emptive strike. It will trigger more, its aim - to prevent a white genocide. Children are legitimate targets as Anders Breivik proved in Norway. Children of invaders do not stay children, they become adults and reproduce, creating more invaders to replace your people. Any alien you kill, of any age, is one less enemy your children will have to face.

Would you rather do the killing or leave it to your children? Your grandchildren.

For once, the person that will be called a fascist is an actual fascist.

There should be a picture of Adolf Hitler in every classroom and every school. Sir Oswald Mosley, leader of the British Union of Fascists, is the person from history closest to my beliefs.

This is my statement. It will be seen and read by millions. I have the platform to speak. No-one can silence me. No-one can drown my voice and my actions.

If I don't survive the attack, goodbye, god bless and I will see you all in Valhalla!

(Tarrant exits and recorded narration follows, with linked moving image)

Actor 4   (recorded voice) On Friday 15 March 2019, Brenton Tarrant donned a helmet mounted GoPro camera, entered the Al Noor Mosque building in Christchurch, New Zealand, and went room-to-room, shooting and killing 42 worshippers.

Tarrant then drove to the Linwood Mosque where he killed another 9 people. On his way to yet another Mosque, police rammed his car and detained him. In total, Facebook removed 1.5 million videos of the attack within the first 24 hours. Tarrant, who was sentenced in 2020, is serving life imprisonment with no parole option.

He quoted Sir Oswald Mosley as his inspiration.

(Blackout and hold that for 10 seconds)

The End

www.ingramcontent.com/pod-product-compliance
Lightning Source LLC
Chambersburg PA
CBHW021120080526
44587CB00010B/585